i ching

i ching

A PRACTICAL GUIDE TO INTERPRETATION AND DIVINATION

will adcock

southwater

This edition is published by Southwater

Distributed in the UK by The Manning Partnership
251–253 London Road East, Batheaston, Bath BA1 7RL, UK
tel. (0044) 01225 852 727   fax (0044) 01225 852 852

Distributed in the USA byOttenheimer Publishing
5 Park Center Court, Suite 300, Owing Mills MD 2117-5001, USA
tel. (001) 410 902 9100   fax (001) 410 902 7210

Distributed in Australia by Sandstone Publishing
Unit 1, 360 Norton Street, Leichhardt, New South Wales 2040, Australia
tel. (0061) 2 9560 7888   fax (0061) 2 9560 7488

Distributed in New Zealand by Five Mile Press NZ
PO Box 33-1071, Takapuna, Auckland 9, New Zealand
tel. (0064) 9 4444 144   fax(0064) 9 4444 518

Southwater is an imprint of Anness Publishing Limited
© 2000 Anness Publishing Limited

1 3 5 7 9 10 8 6 4 2

Publisher: Joanna Lorenz
Senior Editor: Joanne Rippin, *Designer:* Nigel Partridge
Production Controller: Yolande Denny, *Reader:* Richard McGinlay, *Special photography:* Don Last
Illustrators: Rebecca Yue (papercuts) and Anthony Duke

CONTENTS

AN INTRODUCTION TO THE I CHING

≡

*The I Ching has survived
invasions, wars and other
tumultuous cultural upheavals.
It was first devised from observing
the natural world; the ebb and
flow of its cycles. The counsel that
the I Ching offers involves
adopting a more harmonious
approach to life, having an
awareness and a respect for the
influences acting upon us.*

≡

LEFT: *Open your awareness to the changes
that are all around you.*

THE HISTORY OF THE I CHING

People have always sought answers to what might be. Will I be wealthy? Will I achieve my goal? Will I marry? Will I be happy? What is going to happen? It seems to be an intrinsic part of human nature to want to know what the future holds for us, to have an inkling of what might occur in our lives. This is understandable – the future can be a frightening proposition – but there are no absolutes, no Hollywood ending where the final scene shows a beautiful sunset and the protagonists live happily ever after.

Paradoxically, the only certainty in life is change. It is the one constant; day slips into night and night into day. Inorganic elements are transmuted into organic life that progresses through a series of changes, and when that life ends the elements are released and another change is initiated. Spring progresses to summer, summer to autumn, autumn to winter and winter to spring.

BELOW: The vivid colours of autumn supersede the greens of summer as the year progresses.

ABOVE: A carved stone tortoise commemorates the story of the beginnings of the I Ching.

In all change, however, there are certain patterns, and it is this predictability that the shamans of ancient China referred to when they were called upon to give advice and divinations on forthcoming events. These "bamboo shamans" of 4,000 years ago would burn the shoulder blade of an ox or cow, inscribed with the particular question, and divine the answer from the patterns of the cracks that appeared. Later they used tortoise shells in the same manner, the tortoise being revered as a symbol of wisdom and longevity.

RIGHT: A portrait of the learned Emperor, Fu Hsi.

A BLUEPRINT FOR THE UNIVERSE

This method of divination was the origin of the I Ching, which translates as "The Book of Changes". As it developed, it became more than just an oracular device for fortune-telling. The ancient sages began to see that it could be used as a blueprint for understanding the way the whole universe works in all its complexity.

The early stages of the I Ching are shrouded in myth and legend, but the original rendition of the work into written form is credited to the legendary first Emperor of China, Fu Hsi. Fu Hsi was a great sage and scholar. After many years observing and contemplating the natural world and himself, he composed – or, as legend has it, saw on the shell of a tortoise – the eight three-lined diagrams (trigrams) which are the basis of the I Ching. These eight trigrams represented the eight fundamental forces of nature which embody and exemplify the creation that surrounds us, and at some point they were arranged into an octagonal form known as the Pa Kua.

The original Pa Kua was called the "Early Heaven Arrangement" but it was revised at a later date to give a clearer definition of the dynamic interplay of the complementary opposites that work together to produce the changes in creation.

THE DEVELOPMENT OF THE TRIGRAMS

For almost one thousand years, the trigrams were largely untouched, the next transformation being attributed to King Wen, a feudal lord from the province of Chou in western China who was imprisoned by Emperor Chou Hsin. While in prison, King Wen found that by arranging the trigrams in all possible paired combinations they produced 64 different horizontal stacks of six lines (called hexagrams). He also wrote a commentary on the hexagrams that refined the interplay of the energies that each of them symbolized, explaining them, and giving advice on what needed to be looked at in relation to the question that had been asked. After his release, King Wen waged war against Chou Hsin, eventually overthrowing him and founding the Chou dynasty. His son, the Duke of Chou, added another dimension to the 64 hexagrams by giving each line a specific meaning for a deeper insight. Each of the lines are further influenced by yin and yang, which adds another significance to how the hexagram is constructed.

Some 500 years later, the venerable Chinese sage and philosopher Confucius (551-479BC), who valued the I Ching highly, added more observations to the treatise. This gave further weight to an already significant work and extended its popularity as an oracle to be consulted in order to determine a course of action to effect a beneficial change in a situation.

The I Ching did not become widely known in the West until it was translated in the late 19th century by German missionary and Sinologist, Richard Wilhelm. This initial translation into German was readily embraced by the psychologist Carl Gustav Jung, who saw it as confirmation of his theories of synchronicity and the subconscious. An English translation soon followed, and numerous other translations and interpretations have ensured its widespread appeal, giving people from all walks of life advice on problems and self-development.

ABOVE: The eight fundamental trigrams arranged in the Early Heaven Pa Kua.

ABOVE: The venerated sage and philosopher, Confucius, who extended the I Ching's use.

POSITIONING

A hexagram is made up of two separate trigrams – a set of three horizontal lines. The two trigrams maintain individuality in the structure by virtue of their relative positions.

The lower trigram represents the foundation of the situation, and the upper trigram reflects the manner in which the circumstances can develop. In addition to this, each line has its own significance in terms of its position.

• The first line (at the bottom) is related to the early beginnings of a situation, and can be seen as someone of low social standing.

• The second line is where the subject resides, the core of the lower trigram.

• The third line is the transition from the lower trigram to the upper, and is associated with the pitfalls inherent to someone rising above their station without due care.

• The fourth line is seen as the officer, the intermediary between the ruler and the masses. It also signifies a successful rise from the lower trigram to the upper.

• The fifth line represents the ruler, the core of the upper trigram. It can also symbolize good fortune.

• The sixth line indicates that there are things beyond even rulers and is a caution against reaching too high.

RIGHT: Carl Jung felt that the I Ching illustrated his theories of the subconscious.

YIN AND YANG

According to ancient Chinese philosophy, the time before the universe and the earth were created was known as Wu Chi, which means "ultimate nothingness". Out of this formless chaos was born the principle of yin and yang, the fundamental law underlying all of creation. Yin and yang are represented by the Tai Chi, the well-known symbol comprised of a circle divided into two segments, one black and one white. These are the complementary opposites that are apparent in everything; one cannot exist without the other, although they are characterized by extremities that seem to make them poles apart. Where yin is dark, yang is

ABOVE: Dark and light perfectly illustrate the complementary opposites of yin and yang.

light; where yin is soft, yang is hard; where yin is weak, yang is firm; where yin is feminine, yang is masculine; where yin is receptive, yang is active; and so on.

THE UNIFYING PRINCIPLE

The black and white of the Tai Chi describes the polarity of the two forces but it also shows a germinative quality, i.e. each holds within itself the seed of the other. This relates to the principle of constant flux: yang starts from a small point, grows and expands and at its peak transforms into yin, which starts from a small point, transmuting to yang at its zenith, and so the cycle continues. Yin and yang are transient states of being, and it is the interplay of these two elemental energies, or forces, that gives rise to the creation we see

BELOW: The yin qualities of soft, still waters contrast with the hard, yang quality of the wood.

RIGHT: An altar at the Yap Kongsi temple, Penang, China, decorated with the Pa Kua.

around us. A good example of this is a pan of boiling water. As heat is applied, the water near the bottom expands and rises, exhibiting yang qualities; this allows the cooler surface water to sink, which is the yin component; the polarity has now been reversed and what was yin becomes yang, and vice versa.

In a hexagram yin is represented by a broken line, and yang by an unbroken one. The lines are obtained by casting three coins six times. The faces of the coins have values of two (yin) or three (yang), and the sum of the faces will give an even or an odd number which then make up the lines of the hexagram.

BELOW: The yin-yang symbol is a fundamental part of Chinese culture.

YIN	YANG
Moon	Sun
Winter	Summer
Dark	Light
Feminine	Masculine
Interior	Exterior
Low	High
Stillness	Movement
Passive	Active
Even numbers	Odd numbers
Earth	Heaven
Cold	Heat
Soft	Hard
Valleys	Hills
Still water	Mountains
Gardens	Houses

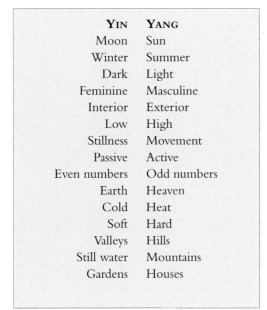

THE DEVELOPMENT OF THE I CHING

It is not known how long ago the philosophy of yin and yang first appeared in written form but the symbols have been in use for millennia. Yang is represented by a single unbroken line and yin by a single broken line:

——— yang (positive)

— — yin (negative)

In this basic form, these symbols can be used in a simple "yes/no" fashion, and a question can be answered with the toss of a coin. Yang is "yes", the "heads" side of the coin, and yin is "no", the "tails" side. However, this system gives no depth of insight into the nature of a situation, no gradation to show what areas can be changed to give a satisfactory outcome.

Yin and yang are very definite – black and white, hard and soft, and so on – and this

BELOW: A 19th-century version of the Pa Kua.

ABOVE: The Pa Kua is often displayed to deflect evil spirits from entering a house or temple.

polarity of opposites was the beginning of a system that could be used to study the workings of the universe and to apply it to aligning humans with the creative principle. Creation is a synergy of the two forces working together and combining to form different structures. It was realized that to give a more tonal quality, to produce the gradation or "shading", further refinement was necessary. To this end, another line was added to each yin or yang, producing four variations which combined the two lines:

═══ yang-yang is yang at its fullest

═ ═ yin-yin is yin at its fullest

═══ yang-yin is rising yang

═══ yin-yang is rising yin

THE CARDINAL DIRECTIONS

These four new symbols gave different strengths to the two basic ones. They were then applied to the four cardinal directions of north, south, east and west, and were arrayed in a square form. They were also seen to be representative of the four seasons and times of day, and the gradation was thus perceived to progress in a natural way:

NORTH/WINTER/MIDNIGHT

WEST/AUTUMN/SUNSET

EAST/SPRING/SUNRISE

SOUTH/SUMMER/NOON

THE EIGHT TRIGRAMS

Further development came with the addition of another line, which produced the eight basic trigrams of the I Ching. These, when combined, give the 64 hexagrams. The eight trigrams were given specific names taken from nature and arranged in the Pa Kua, showing opposing pairs of forces. The trigrams are read from the bottom upwards or from the centre of the Pa Kua outwards. The trigrams were given attributes and characteristics that define them symbolically in terms of the natural world, human social arrangements, colours, animal totems and body parts, to name just a few. In an I Ching consultation, these images are used metaphorically to give depth and refinement to the hexagrams they make.

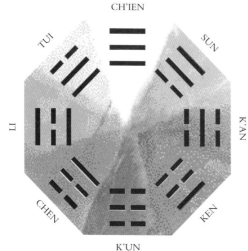

CH'IEN
TUI
SUN
LI
K'AN
CHEN
KEN
K'UN

THE EIGHT FORCES

CH'IEN/HEAVEN

CHEN/THUNDER

K'UN/EARTH

SUN/WIND

LI/FIRE

KEN/MOUNTAIN

K'AN/WATER

TUI/LAKE

CASTING WITH YARROW STALKS

The traditional method of consulting the I Ching was to use yarrow stalks. As with the coins, the yarrow stalks were treated with great respect and kept in a safe place. Using yarrow stalks took longer than using coins and therefore required concentration to be held for longer, but there was an advantage in this because holding concentration for extended periods gives rise to a more altered state which allows for a greater receptivity. Also, because it takes longer, the consulter was less likely to seek guidance in a lackadaisical or hurried manner and was more likely to give their actions the attention they deserve.

A set consisted of 50 stalks. Before the consultation began, one stalk was removed from the bundle to leave 49. The stalks were then randomly divided into two piles representing the two primal forces of yang and yin. One stalk was taken from the pile on the right and held between the little and ring fingers of the left hand. Stalks were then removed from the left-hand pile in groups of four, a number representative of change as exhibited by the four seasons. This process was repeated until there were only one, two, three or four stalks

remaining, and these were placed between the third and fourth fingers of the left hand. The same was done with the right-hand pile, the stalks left being placed between the index and middle fingers. These stalks were put aside and the same method was followed with the bundle another two times to give three piles of stalks which, when added together, gave the first line of the hexagram: yin, yang, old yin or old yang. The whole process was repeated a further five times to get the other lines and so construct the hexagram.

RIGHT: The use of yarrow stalks predates the use of coins.

THE CHARACTERISTICS OF THE TRIGRAMS

CH'IEN represents heaven, the creative. In the family it is the father, and in the body the head. It is strong and active, the three yang lines representing limitless potential and endurance. Its colour is white and its animal is the horse. It also symbolizes ice and the fruit of a tree.

K'UN represents earth, the receptive. The family member is the mother; the body part is the belly. It is gentle and passive, the three yin lines representing endless nurturing and devotion. Its colour is black and its animal is the cow. It also symbolizes the tree trunk, and a cart, carrying without distinction.

CHEN represents thunder, the arousing. In the family it is the eldest son, and in the body the foot. It is violent and determined, full of spontaneity and excitement. Its colour is bright red and its animal the dragon, symbol of speed and power. It represents the fast-growing reed, volcanoes and earthquakes.

SUN represents wind, the gentle and penetrating. In the family it is the eldest daughter, and in the body the thighs. It is soothing, persevering and just, characterizing flexibility and strength. Its colour is lush green and its animal is the cat or tiger. It also symbolizes tall, graceful trees such as the willow that can bend before the wind and spring back easily.

K'AN represents water, the abysmal. In the family it is the middle son, and the body part is the ear. It is dangerous and fearless, full of hidden perils and swirling, erosive forces. Its colour is deep blue and its animal the pig or boar. It is also symbolic of marrowy wood, soft and spongy, able to soak up water but lacking great strength.

 LI represents fire, the clinging. In the family it is the middle daughter, and in the body the eyes. It is bright, warm and clear, corresponding to beauty and intelligence. Its colour is warm orange and its animal is the peacock. Li also represents dry, brittle trees.

 KEN represents the mountain, the stillness. The family member is the youngest son, and the body part the hand. It is calm, meditative and earnest, able to withdraw yet to grasp firmly. Its colour is purple and its animal the dog. It is seen as a hermit and as a strong, twisted tree on a mountainside.

 TUI represents the lake, the joyful. In the family it is the youngest daughter, and in the body the mouth and lips. Tender and sensual on the outside, making it attractive and inviting, it possesses a hard, iron core. Its colour is yellow; its animal is the sheep. It also represents a sorceress, mist and harvests.

HOW TO USE I CHING

Observe a tree. It grows when conditions are favourable for growth, and it withdraws and stores its strength when they are not. It bends before the wind for it knows that the wind is stronger than it; for the time being. Be as a tree: grow when you can and save your strength for when you cannot; bend before the superior force but be ready to spring back.

LEFT: *Study the natural world, learn by its example and adopt its harmony.*

CONSULTING THE ORACLE

The I Ching does not tell you, the consulter, what to do. It advises, it counsels on the nature of a problem and the best way to deal with it. It is the Sage that is aware of all possibilities, and the insights it offers are pertinent to you and your situation. The onus of effecting the change is on you accepting the advice and acting on it. For a consultation several things are needed, both physical and metaphysical:

- a calm, reflective state of mind
- a question to ask
- a pad and pen
- three coins

LEFT: Three Chinese coins; the yang side is more heavily inscribed.

relax and focus your intent. The following techniques are suggestions for improving a meditative state, or alternatively you may want to make up your own little ceremony or ritual.

- Light a candle and contemplate the flame. A living flame is beautiful, and as you give it your attention imagine it illuminating you inside.
- Burn some incense. The calming effects of incense have been used for thousands of years, and the smoke also has cleansing properties. As you

RITUAL

The most important factors to bring to an I Ching consultation are an open mind and humility. That is not to say that it is necessary to prostrate yourself, but you do need to leave your ego at the door in order to show proper respect to a wise and venerated Sage. In fact, the humility has already begun because you have taken the first steps in approaching the oracle for advice, recognizing as you do this that you have a need for assistance or counsel and that there is a higher power that you can call upon.

As an aid to achieving a calm and receptive state of mind when approaching the I Ching, it is useful to perform a small ritual to help you

BELOW: Light a candle and contemplate its flame to help with inner illumination.

Essentially, when consulting the I Ching, you are circumventing the conscious mind and all the hormones and emotions that have such a large effect on it, and contacting the higher self. This is the part of you which is in direct communication with the rest of creation, the part of you through which intuition flows and which wants only what is best for you. With time and practice it will become easier to reach a calm state of mind and it may be that after a while a ritual is unnecessary, although it does serve to differentiate the consultation from the day-to-day life that you are seeking help with.

FORMULATING A QUESTION

What is it you are consulting the I Ching about? What are you seeking guidance on? It is necessary to first determine the subject so that you can pose the question in such a way that is unambiguous. It is then necessary to approach the subject with the seriousness it deserves. The I Ching is not a party game and will not respond to frivolous questions or if you are indifferent to the counsel it offers.

Some people consult the I Ching on a daily basis concerning the best way to act on that day; others only consult it at times of crisis or when at a crossroads in life. The frequency is not important, but if you ask too often it is a sign that you are probably not relaxed. Don't repeat questions because that indicates that you have no faith in the answer you first received; this may lead to the

ABOVE: A calm, reflective state of mind is needed for a consultation; take time to focus yourself.

watch the smoke, imagine it gently pervading your aura, purifying it of any negative energies that you may have accumulated.
• Breathe deeply and slowly from your diaphragm for a few breaths. This helps you to relax and focus your attention.
• Pass the coins through the incense smoke to purify them. The effects of the smoke will also cleanse the auras of nearby objects and places.

Sage withdrawing its assistance and further answers you receive will be confused or garbled. Whatever the impetus for the consultation, it is the manner in which it is approached that is important. It should always be the same — detached, relaxed and focused.

• Try and maintain an objective, detached attitude. If you are emotionally involved in the question, and if it is of great importance to you when you ask it, the charged nature of your physical state will interfere with the clarity of the process. In an emotional state you will also be less receptive to the answer you receive because it may not be the one you were hoping for.
• Write the question down, preferably in a journal or notebook in which you can also record the lines as you construct a hexagram. Writing the question down helps to clarify it in your mind, making it easier to focus on it and enabling you to refer back to it at a later date if you wish.
• Take a few moments to meditate on the question while you hold the coins quietly in your hands before you cast them.

Another way to formulate a question is to hold in your mind the image of the situation or person with which you want guidance as you hold the coins. This is especially useful if the matter is complex and the question is likely to be wordy. Writing it down in such a case could then follow the form of "What is the best way to proceed?"

ABOVE: Record your questions and answers in a special journal that is kept for this purpose.

or "How should I deal with this?"

The hexagrams obtained by casting coins or yarrow stalks can take one of two forms:
• The lines may be young yin and young yang and remain unchanged;
• Changing lines (old yin and old yang) mean a second hexagram is constructed. (See overleaf).

COINS AND THEIR VALUES

A physical way of constructing a hexagram is needed, and the most common is to throw or cast three coins. The coins can be of any denomination but it is best to use ones of the same size and value. If you can get some, old Chinese coins are satisfying to use because of their symbolic connection with the I Ching. They are round with a square hole in the middle – the circularity represents the principle of yang, the infinite creativity of heaven, while the square hole represents the principle of yin, the measurable area of the receptive earth.

Once you have chosen some coins, it is best to use the same ones for casting and not to let any-

BELOW: Care for your coins and keep them in a safe place out of the way.

ABOVE: Hold the coins for a moment in your hand before you throw them, as you would throw dice.

one else touch them because, as with anything, their auras can be influenced by energies from another source. Treat them with care and respect because they are an important link to the Sage. Traditionally, the coins were blessed and purified then stored with the I Ching on a shelf above shoulder height, only to be moved for the purposes of a consultation.

The faces of the coins are assigned a value, which when added together give a total to determine whether a line of a hexagram will be yin or yang. The "heads" side (the more heavily inscribed side on a Chinese coin) is considered yang and is valued at three, while the "tails" side is yin and given a value of two. When the coins are thrown a total of six, seven, eight or nine is obtained, giving lines that are either yin (even numbers) or yang (odd numbers).

CONSTRUCTING A HEXAGRAM

The aim of casting the coins is to construct one of the 64 hexagrams which will give you the counsel of the I Ching. The process is very simple and doesn't take long to do, but you will find it beneficial to take some time to prepare yourself; a successful interpretation will depend on how receptive you are as well as on the wisdom of the I Ching.

First prepare yourself mentally as described before. Take a few moments to find a comfortable position, perform a simple ritual to focus your mind, and breathe deeply and slowly to relax. Now write down your question and focus on it for a few moments. Purify your coins and then hold them in your hand while you focus on what you seek guidance on, then shake them gently in your cupped hands while concentrating on the question.

When you feel that it is the right moment, drop the coins on to a hard surface such as a table or the floor and add up the values of the faces. Remember that odd numbers give yang lines and even numbers give yin lines. Repeat this process a further five times until you have six totals. The first total makes up the first line, which lies at the bottom of the hexagram. The hexagram is constructed upwards, following the path of organic growth.

LEFT: Concentrate for a moment on your question before casting.

Once the hexagram is obtained, it can be identified by looking at the Table of Trigrams. The left-hand side of the table shows the lower trigrams, and the top of the table shows the upper trigrams. Find the component trigrams of the hexagram you have constructed and the square where they meet will give the number of the hexagram. Once you have that number, turn to the relevant page in The Hexagrams setion and read the interpretation of it. In the example below, the lower trigram is Ch'ien and the upper is K'un. Looking at the Table of Trigrams, we can see that combined they produce hexagram number 11, T'ai (Peace).

In the following example, x denotes "heads" (3) and - denotes "tails" (2). If you throw only sevens and eights, it indicates that the answer is very clear and you need only read the interpretation of the relevant hexagram.

Sixth throw:	x x -	= 8	
Fifth throw:	x x -	= 8	K'un
Fourth throw:	x x -	= 8	
Third throw:	x - -	= 7	
Second throw:	x - -	= 7	Ch'ien
First throw:	x - -	= 7	

CHANGING LINES

The totals of the coins' faces can produce two odd numbers and two even numbers. The seven and the eight stay the same. The six and the nine, however, represent old yin and old yang which means that they are at their extremes, so each changes to its opposite.

SIX is old yin, written thus, and becomes young yang. —x—

SEVEN is young yang, written thus, and stays the same. ———

EIGHT is young yin, written thus, and stays the same. — —

NINE is old yang, written thus, and becomes young yin. —●—

The changing lines give deeper insights into a reading. The initial hexagram relates to present conditions; the changing lines produce a second hexagram which relates to the future outcome of a situation or helps to clarify the original question. If you receive a hexagram with changing lines, read the interpretation of the first hexagram and the lines that are changing, then go to the second hexagram and read the interpretation only.

RIGHT: Purifying the coins in the smoke from burning incense is part of the ritual of casting.

The following example shows changing lines:

Sixth throw:	= 9 —●—	becomes	— —
Fifth throw:	= 7 ———	becomes	———
Fourth throw:	= 8 — —	becomes	— —
Third throw:	= 8 — —	becomes	— —
Second throw:	= 6 —x—	becomes	———
First throw:	= 7 ———	becomes	———

The first throw produced hexagram number 42 I (Increase), with lines two and six changing, which then gave hexagram number 60 Chieh (Limitation). Going to the relevant page, you would read the interpretation and lines two and six of I, then you would go to Chieh and read the interpretation only.

INTERPRETING

To benefit from the interpretation you need to keep the same open, detached mind. Read the text carefully. It may be useful to note down your immediate responses or thoughts relating to the interpretation. If you feel that the answers are unclear, it could mean that you didn't phrase the question with sufficient clarity or that you are not in a receptive enough state of mind. Leave it and come back to it later.

TABLE OF TRIGRAMS

	CH'IEN	CHEN	K'AN	KEN	TUI	LI	SUN	K'UN
CH'IEN	1	34	5	26	43	14	9	11
CHEN	25	51	3	27	17	21	42	24
K'AN	6	40	29	4	47	64	59	7
KEN	33	62	39	52	31	56	53	15
TUI	10	54	60	41	58	38	61	19
LI	13	55	63	22	49	30	37	36
SUN	44	32	48	18	28	50	57	46
K'UN	12	16	8	23	45	35	20	2

LOWER TRIGRAMS

TABLE OF HEXAGRAMS

	CH'IEN	CHEN	K'AN	KEN	TUI	LI	SUN	K'UN
CH'IEN								
CHEN								
K'AN								
KEN								
TUI								
LI								
SUN								
K'UN								

THE HEXAGRAMS

*Once you have cast the coins, use
the Table of Trigrams to find out
which hexagram you have been
given. If you have changing lines,
read the interpretation and the
lines you received for the initial
hexagram before going on to
read the interpretation of
the second one.*

LEFT: *Be inspired by the grace and harmony
of the natural world.*

乾

1. CH'IEN

THE CREATIVE

Masculine, dynamic, inspiring, stamina, overbearing

HEAVEN

HEAVEN

Heaven over heaven represents the ceaseless creative force of the universe that is available to you if you follow the proper principles. If you are true to yourself and release old habits, you will allow the superior qualities of humility, patience, acceptance and tolerance to grow. Be strong and true, and the energy of creation will flow through you, unfolding your destiny in a propitious manner and leading to great things. Persevere in trusting that the unknowable workings of fate are only serving to bring you the lessons you need to grow stronger, and to retain your inner truth as you go from strength to strength.

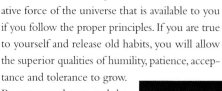

LINE READINGS

6 Retain your humility and acceptance, or you will be in danger of suffering a great fall.

5 Do not struggle on alone. Join with other like-minded people and work together for the mutual benefit of all.

4 Trust in your inner truth to guide you, and do not hesitate in making a choice.

3 Keep a sense of perspective and do not let adulation go to your head.

2 The best way to exert an influence is to lead others by good example.

1 Be patient and listen to what your heart says. It will tell you when to act.

坤

2. K'UN

THE RECEPTIVE

Feminine, yielding, receptive, gentle, providing, bountiful

EARTH

EARTH

This is the complement to the first hexagram. For the creative to take root and flourish, it needs receptive ground to provide nourishment. Cultivate the yielding, receptive nature that will provide the appropriate ground for the seeds of wisdom to grow. The image of the earth is the endless provider, giving without complaint and without seeking recognition. This is the time to follow because there is not sufficient experience to lead or initiate change. Concentrate upon developing your inner strength so that what you receive now will produce bountiful results in the future.

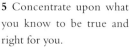

LINE READINGS

6 Remain passive but be open and receptive; be guided by the wisdom of the Sage.

5 Concentrate upon what you know to be true and right for you.

4 Keep yourself to yourself and be reserved in both your actions and your words.

3 Be inspired by others but do not trumpet your own achievements.

2 Respond to circumstances as they arise with suppleness and adaptability.

1 Take some time to consolidate what you learn and to work on developing your inner truth.

屯
3. CHUN
DIFFICULT BEGINNINGS
Greenness, immaturity, new growth, sprouting, perseverance

WATER

THUNDER

This is a time of potential growth, of new beginnings, but like any new venture there is often initial adversity. Just as the seedling perseveres and grows, so too will you overcome difficult beginnings if you patiently persevere in holding on to proper principles. A new situation can develop in any direction, and by being aware of this possibility you will be able to correct harmful growth before it goes too far. Accept any help that is offered to you and try to remain steadfast during this chaotic time. If you allow the situation to resolve itself your progress will be successful.

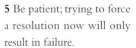
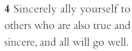
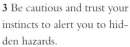

LINE READINGS

6 Trust in the guidance of the I Ching and you will win through eventually.

5 Be patient; trying to force a resolution now will only result in failure.

4 Sincerely ally yourself to others who are also true and sincere, and all will go well.

3 Be cautious and trust your instincts to alert you to hidden hazards.

2 Don't compromise; wait patiently for a solution that is correct in all respects, not just one.

1 Progress is difficult but be patient and the way ahead will become apparent eventually.

蒙
4. MENG
YOUTHFUL FOLLY
Inexperience, guidance, enthusiasm, tuition

MOUNTAIN

WATER

Youth is a time of inexperience but not necessarily a lack of years; it is possible to be old yet inexperienced in a certain subject or area. Youth is also a time of boundless enthusiasm which can lead to folly but, by its very nature, enthusiasm can also see us through the setbacks that inexperience can cause. This beginner's luck will eventually run out, however, and Mêng counsels that to continue to grow it is necessary to seek guidance from an experienced teacher and to learn from our own mistakes. The I Ching offers this guidance, and its wisdom can help us to learn as we grow.

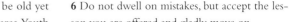
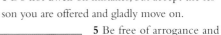
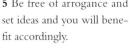
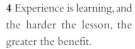
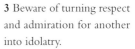
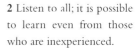
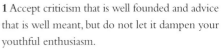

LINE READINGS

6 Do not dwell on mistakes, but accept the lesson you are offered and gladly move on.

5 Be free of arrogance and set ideas and you will benefit accordingly.

4 Experience is learning, and the harder the lesson, the greater the benefit.

3 Beware of turning respect and admiration for another into idolatry.

2 Listen to all; it is possible to learn even from those who are inexperienced.

1 Accept criticism that is well founded and advice that is well meant, but do not let it dampen your youthful enthusiasm.

5. HSU

WAITING

*Correctness, patience,
perseverance, nourishment*

WATER

HEAVEN

There is a time for advancement and a time for patient non-action. Now is the time to wait and have faith in the order of things. The image of this hexagram is of clouds gathering before rain can fall. The clouds are the creative potential of the universe, which will bring nourishment to the land when the time is right. To gather this creative energy it is necessary to wait with the correct attitude of calm patience, persevering in maintaining the inner truth that will allow the universe to work. Use this time to observe yourself and your situation, and correct any inferior feelings that only serve to cause imbalance.

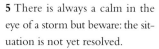

LINE READINGS

6 The situation is coming to a resolution, although it is perhaps not as you had wished or hoped for; accept your fate with humility.

5 There is always a calm in the eye of a storm but beware: the situation is not yet resolved.

4 Remain calm and confident that things are as they should be.

3 Do not give in to your inner doubts but wait with calmness and self-discipline.

2 Keep your self-discipline and do not respond to attacks that may come from others.

1 An outside influence is approaching. Prepare yourself by remaining calm and focused.

---

6. SUNG

CONFLICT

*Opposition, disengagement,
communication*

HEAVEN

WATER

Conflict arises from within, and the strong connection to heaven is being eroded by the swirling confusion of water. By trying to impose your view instead of accepting what comes, you are in conflict with the universe, and this attracts external opposition. This clash cannot be overcome by force or aggression as confrontation only serves to feed the ego. Disengage from doubts, fears and impatience, and instead communicate with others to develop an understanding that will help to resolve the conflict. Accept and respect the advice of someone wiser than you in this situation.

LINE READINGS

6 Conflict gives rise to more conflict. In the long run it is better just to let it go.

5 Accept the wisdom of an objective third party and things will work out well.

4 Stay calm and resolved and recognize the pointlessness of conflict.

3 By retaining your integrity and humility you can achieve great things.

2 Calmly pulling back from conflict will bring benefits to all involved.

1 A difficult situation is in danger of escalating. Defuse it now before it is too late and gets out of hand.

7. SHIH

THE ARMY

Unity, harmony, acting in concert, strength, division

EARTH

WATER

There is dissent in the ranks, causing unrest and instability. This is because the leader is overbearing, unjust or weak-willed. For an army to function well it needs a strong leader who commands respect with a balance of compassion, strength and wisdom. You are an army but you are divided within because your general is not leading by example. This lack of inner harmony brings disunity to other relationships because you are acting from an unstable position. Be firm in your purpose and exemplary in your actions and you will be an inspiration to others, gaining their support and achieving a worthy goal.

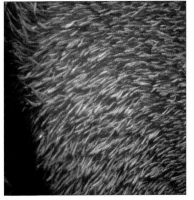

LINE READINGS

6 Success is yours, but rather than celebrating, reflect honestly on how it was gained.

5 Retaliation against disruptive elements should be done with restraint and understanding.

4 Unless you are working coherently within yourself or with others there can be no advancement.

3 Maintain your honesty and integrity and a realistic sense of authority.

2 It is the mutual support between the leader and followers that carries the day.

1 Retain your sense of justice and take care to behave correctly at all times.

---

8. PI

HOLDING TOGETHER

Union, bonding, co-operation

WATER

EARTH

This hexagram suggests harmony, the water soaking into the earth to produce a good harvest. Any union needs to be harmonious for the best results, whether the relationship is with yourself or with others. Now is a good time for strengthening those bonds by reviewing your actions and demeanour. Are you being truthful? You are in a position of power but that doesn't mean that you can do what you like. However, it does require steadiness of principle in the face of challenges and temptations. Maintain your inner truth and sincerity and you will achieve much.

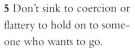
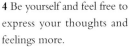

LINE READINGS

6 Proceed cautiously but do not hesitate to enter a beneficial union when the opportunity comes.

5 Don't sink to coercion or flattery to hold on to someone who wants to go.

4 Be yourself and feel free to express your thoughts and feelings more.

3 Be wary of joining in with a group of people who may lead you astray.

2 Do not be swayed by inferior principles in yourself or others just to keep the image of harmony.

1 Lack of truth, in yourself or with others, will inevitably lead to disunity.

小畜

9. HSIAO CH'U

THE TAMING POWER OF
THE SMALL

Patience, yielding, strength

WIND

HEAVEN

Others recognize who you are and what you stand for, but not sufficiently to allow trouble-free advancement. You could force your way but that is beneath you and will only bring misfortune. The only way to progress is to remain focused on your path and to seek to remove obstacles with gentle actions. Look to the long term rather than to immediate satisfaction; by planting the correct seeds now you will reap a richer harvest in the future. Cultivate patience, tolerance, adaptability and detachment, and accept that all you can do is change yourself.

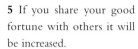
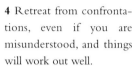
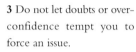

LINE READINGS

6 Success is imminent. Adhere to the correct principles and its arrival is assured.

5 If you share your good fortune with others it will be increased.

4 Retreat from confrontations, even if you are misunderstood, and things will work out well.

3 Do not let doubts or over-confidence tempt you to force an issue.

2 Remain firm and devoted to your inner truth and all will come right.

1 Impatience causes despair and hasty actions, which will not benefit you.

履

10. LU

CONDUCT

*Caution, courtesy,
simplicity, innocence*

HEAVEN

LAKE

The allusion in this hexagram is to stepping on a tiger's tail, in other words overstepping the mark and causing offence. The things to be aware of in this instance are caution and restraint, but do not confuse wariness with hesitation. If you conduct yourself with humility and good humour, it is possible to walk on the most dangerous ground with a degree of safety. By maintaining simplicity of thought and deed, and innocent expression of your inner truth, others will accept you for who you are. Do not be subservient to those above nor domineering to those below and you will be able to move with confidence, and therefore meet with success.

LINE READINGS

6 True achievement is measured in the manner of attainment as well as in the rewards gained.

5 Be resolute and determined with yourself but not hard and judgemental with others.

4 Do not be tempted to avert or interfere with a difficult situation; just leave it alone.

3 Don't over-estimate yourself or your abilities, but instead allow things to develop as they will.

2 You know what is correct; doubts and questions will only cloud the issue and bring trouble.

1 Step lightly with quiet confidence and without ambition to ensure smooth progress.

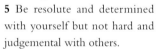

11. T'AI

PEACE

Balance, harmony,
new growth, prosperity

EARTH

HEAVEN

Your inner harmony is reflected in the peace that surrounds you. This hexagram is in perfect balance: earth above indicates an open attitude to events, and heaven below suggests a time of burgeoning potential. In such fertile ground it is possible to grow to great heights but you need to maintain the inner balance that has brought about this situation. Most spiritual growth comes through challenging times and T'ai serves as a reminder not to relax into complacency just because times are good. To develop the new growth potential of this period you need to remain devoted to the correct principles of the I Ching.

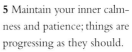

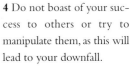

LINE READINGS

6 Good fortune fades, to be replaced by a time of learning. Accept what comes calmly.

5 Maintain your inner calmness and patience; things are progressing as they should.

4 Do not boast of your success to others or try to manipulate them, as this will lead to your downfall.

3 Keep your equanimity in difficult times because times will change.

2 Be generous and forbearing and do not allow your good fortune to cloud your judgement.

1 Others are attracted by your positivity. Welcome them and act together.

---

12. P'I

STANDSTILL

Lack of progress,
barriers, stagnation

HEAVEN

EARTH

A difficult time is coming. P'i is the reverse of the previous hexagram, indicating that the creative is leaving and the receptive is rising. This is as inevitable as the progression of the seasons; the run of good fortune has waned and now comes the change to a time of stagnation. This lack of progress does not mean that you cannot develop your inner truth. Be receptive to the lessons and don't struggle against those who hold the upper hand because that will only serve to make them stronger. Retreat into yourself and have faith that things will improve quicker if you persevere in the correct manner.

LINE READINGS

6 By acting with a pure heart and honest intent you will meet with good fortune.

5 Adhere to your higher principles to strengthen your inner truth.

4 Acting in a pure and simple manner will bring benefits to all and support from others.

3 Make no judgements of others but do what you know to be right.

2 Times are hard but the best way to proceed is by enduring with patience and trust.

1 Withdraw from an adverse situation and wait patiently for better times.

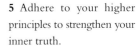

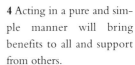

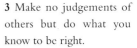

同人
13. T'UNG JEN

FELLOWSHIP WITH OTHERS

*Cohesion, bonding, strength in
numbers, co-operation*

HEAVEN

FIRE

This hexagram speaks of a union of equals coming together to work towards a mutual goal, with no reservations or hidden agendas. To function coherently requires openness, honesty and a sense of fairness felt by all. By the same token, if there are reservations within elements of the group it will not work. These reservations need to be addressed if you are to continue or else a state of chaos will prevail and nothing will be achieved. This hexagram also refers to joining with the Sage, being sincerely committed to seeking the wisdom and truth without regard to having it proven to ourselves.

LINE READINGS

6 Good fortune will come if you whole-heartedly embrace the wisdom of the Sage.

5 Bonds based on love and respect are unbreakable, and reconciliation will come in its own time.

4 Misunderstandings lead to trouble. It is better to disengage than to continue fighting.

3 Feelings of mistrust will grow and break the union unless dealt with quickly.

2 Creation of factions within the group will lead to failure.

1 For a union to endure there needs to be openness between the parties involved.

大有
14. TA YU

POSSESSING PLENTY

*Feminine, yielding, receptive,
gentle, providing, bountiful*

FIRE

HEAVEN

By following true and honest intentions you are entering a period of great abundance. This is a powerful position in which you can shine like a fire in the heavens. The weak yin line in the position of the leader indicates that you have reached this point by retaining your humility and integrity. Carry on in this manner and you will continue to rise and prosper, becoming a guiding light for others. Because of your strong position it is important that you guard against unworthy thoughts and actions or seeking to use your influence to further your own ends. If you abuse your strength it will be lost to you.

LINE READINGS

6 If you continue with modesty and humility great abundance will come.

5 Do not be effusive or stand-offish but accept people with a quiet dignity.

4 Rise above petty competition and you will continue on your ascent.

3 Do not hoard your wealth, spiritual or material, because that leads to stagnation.

2 Remain free of attachments because possessions can become fetters.

1 Do not allow your integrity to be waylaid by feelings of arrogance or superiority as your good fortune continues.

15. CH'IEN

MODESTY

*Quietly progressing, steadfast,
deepening, developing*

EARTH

MOUNTAIN

Strive to remain modest in your dealings with others and yourself. The image of the mountain below the earth is one of curtailing ostentatious behaviour to deepen and develop the inner self. Modesty is more than a lack of boastfulness or curbing a sense of superiority; it is also about perceiving what is good and right, and being steadfast in acting upon it and following those actions through. If you maintain such an awareness and follow the correct path, deeper contact with the Sage and with your inner truth is forged, strengthening you and enabling you to face any obstacles with calm confidence.

LINE READINGS

6 A truly modest person has the wisdom to know what is right and the strength to follow it.

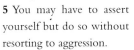

5 You may have to assert yourself but do so without resorting to aggression.

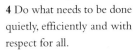

4 Do what needs to be done quietly, efficiently and with respect for all.

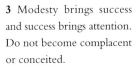

3 Modesty brings success and success brings attention. Do not become complacent or conceited.

2 Others recognize and appreciate a deep modesty in you and will react accordingly.

1 True modesty brings its own rewards. Do not expect or seek recognition for your actions.

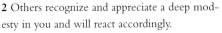

---

16. YU

ENTHUSIASM

Energy, opportunity, support

THUNDER

EARTH

This is a good time to start a new undertaking, but be sure your foundations are strong. Your boundless enthusiasm provides the energy and strength to see it through, and the strong yang line in the position of the leader indicates that your vigour will communicate to others, who will join with you and lend their support. However, the enthusiasm needs to be derived from a strong inner clarity of what is right and what needs to be done. If it springs from an egotistical desire to simply be seen to be successful and prosperous, you will become unbalanced and the energy will not be sufficient to carry you through.

LINE READINGS

6 Enthusiasm springing from the desires of the ego will lead to eventual misfortune.

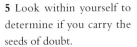

5 Look within yourself to determine if you carry the seeds of doubt.

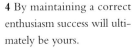

4 By maintaining a correct enthusiasm success will ultimately be yours.

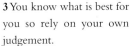

3 You know what is best for you so rely on your own judgement.

2 Be sensible in your goals; retain a sense of propriety and a realistic view of what can be done.

1 Acting in an arrogant manner will alienate others and will prove to be your undoing. Therefore cultivate a modest demeanour.

17. SUI

FOLLOWING

Acceptance, following, joy

LAKE

THUNDER

A fundamental principle of the I Ching is an acceptance of the way things are while maintaining equanimity in response to events. This hexagram relates to following and being followed. The arousing thunder is rising to the joyous lake. In the same manner the principles of the I Ching arouse the interest of a follower and adherence to the principles of humility, inner truth and acceptance will lead to joy. Other people will see the joy in a true follower and, in turn, their interest is aroused. To show them the way to true joy you must remain steadfast to the principles of the Sage, the I Ching.

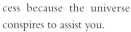

LINE READINGS

6 Being receptive to the principles of the Sage brings what is needed at the right time.

5 By being true to yourself you ensure great success because the universe conspires to assist you.

4 Do not let flattery go to your head or your clarity will become clouded.

3 It may be time to part company from people or ideas that are not true to your inner knowledge.

2 Inferior attitudes will prevent you hearing wisdom from truly wise people and from the Sage.

1 Wisdom can come from unexpected sources. Be respectful to all and listen carefully.

18. KU

WORK ON CORRUPTION

Disruption, decay, disorder, spoiled, repairing

MOUNTAIN

WIND

This ideogram represents decay and corruption. The hexagram itself portrays the penetrating wind blowing around the base of the mountain, which indicates the deep-rootedness of the disorder. However, there is a chance to redeem the situation by correcting the improper attitudes and ideas, thus changing the disruption to a state of harmony. This will take strength of character and decisive action, but first it is necessary to ascertain the root cause, which requires a period of meditation and introspection. Once established, work quickly to repair the damage and guard against its return.

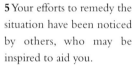

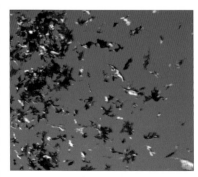

LINE READINGS

6 Following the path of inner truth may isolate you but this will not be permanent.

5 Your efforts to remedy the situation have been noticed by others, who may be inspired to aid you.

4 Deal with evident corruption now to avoid any further disruption.

3 An excessive approach has led to a minor upset but no great harm has been done.

2 Use gentle persistence to address the decay. Excessive vigour will lead to further disruption.

1 Decay in this case is coming from a pattern learned rather than from an inner voice.

19. LIN

APPROACH

Advance, waxing power,
strength, benevolence

EARTH

LAKE

This hexagram refers to what is approaching you and how you approach life. There are good times coming imminently and any undertaking you begin will be successful. This is because you have cultivated the correct internal equanimity to approach events in a balanced and detached manner. By adopting this attitude, the higher powers approach you to give assistance. But just because times are good it doesn't mean that you can relax the inner discipline that has brought about the success. If you do, the progress that has begun will halt and your good fortune will melt away.

LINE READINGS

6 You have reached a point in your spiritual development where you are able to help others.

5 Don't interfere or have doubts about the abilities of those helping you.

4 An open-minded attitude towards others will ensure your success.

3 Keep your attitudes to yourself and keep other people under control to ensure continued progress.

2 The correct approach will help you through the bad times that inevitably follow the good times.

1 Fortunate circumstances make your progress seem effortless, but maintain your discipline.

---

20. KUAN

CONTEMPLATION

Meditation, understanding,
perceiving, example

WIND

EARTH

By contemplating or meditating upon the principles of the I Ching, those attributes become a part of our make-up. Once this perspective has been attained, the bearer becomes a guiding light that is apparent for all to see. The creative power of the universe also works in unseen ways, influencing situations and people without conscious intent like ripples spreading on a pond. This position of strength has been attained by perseverance in adhering to the inner correctness outlined by the Sage. It allows the universal energy to flow through and to transmute the petty aspects of the self into tolerance, patience and understanding.

LINE READINGS

6 Your contemplation has achieved the desired results in yourself.

5 Contemplation furthers your understanding but only becomes wisdom when put into practice.

4 Your wisdom can have a positive influence on others but do not force your opinions on them.

3 Trust your feelings. You have enough self-awareness to recognize when improper responses to life arise.

2 Do not expect to make great leaps forward. Gradual progress is inexorable and long-lasting.

1 Just because you follow the teachings of the Sage you cannot expect others to do so.

21. SHIH HO

BITING THROUGH

Clarity, decisiveness, obstacle, unity

FIRE

THUNDER

The yang line in the fourth position represents an obstruction which is preventing a mouth from closing properly to allow nourishment. There is an obstacle here, which could be an incorrect attitude in you or in someone else, that needs to be dealt with now. It will not go away of its own accord so what is needed is clarity to see the problem and decisiveness of action to "bite"

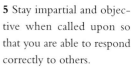

through it. This does not mean using aggressive force because an overly robust response will bring misfortune. Instead, it is necessary to return to the principles of correctness as laid out in the I Ching. Use your inner strength to withdraw.

LINE READINGS

6 If you persist stubbornly in dealing with the situation, severe misfortune will result.

5 Stay impartial and objective when called upon so that you are able to respond correctly to others.

4 You begin to see progress in dealing with the problem. Maintain your balance.

3 You are faced with an old problem. The correct way to deal with it this time is to withdraw.

2 In responding to the obstruction, you may have gone too far but there is no great harm done.

1 This is a new obstacle, a first offence. Be lenient in how you deal with it.

---

22. PI

GRACE

Adornment, beauty, simplicity

MOUNTAIN

FIRE

Grace is perfect poise, beauty and balance. True grace comes from a firm inner truth, humility and acceptance, whereas false grace relies on external appearances to beautify the self for the appeasement of the ego. Grace is the embodiment of nature and possesses a beauty that is effortless; a mountain bathed in the light of the setting sun does not try to be beautiful but is breathtaking nevertheless. Similarly, a person who does not try to be alluring but cultivates devotion to the

simplicity of the inner truth of the Sage possesses a grace and beauty that shines through the dowdiest of coverings.

LINE READINGS

6 The external trappings of success are false. True power and grace shine from within.

5 Concentrate on simplicity and sincerity and don't allow yourself to be tempted to seek material wealth.

4 Do not try to impress others with an outward show of brilliance.

3 All seems well but be careful not to fall into complacency and arrogance.

2 Cultivate an ability to see through surface adornment to perceive the underlying integrity.

1 Let modesty and your own integrity be your guide to inner truth.

23. PO
SPLITTING APART
Strong, enduring, patient,
non-action

MOUNTAIN

EARTH

Everything seems to be going horribly wrong, but nothing can be done about it except to batten down the hatches and weather the storm. To attempt to influence the situation will only prolong it because such a desire is driven by the ego, which seeks to dominate and control. Acting on the imperatives of the ego causes the splitting apart, so by withdrawing from the unfavourable circumstances and engaging in patient non-action the creative power is allowed free rein to settle the situation favourably. Be like the mountain, strong and immovable, resting solidly on the earth of your proper principles.

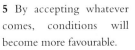

LINE READINGS

6 Do not dwell on what has passed but step forward with optimism into better times.

5 By accepting whatever comes, conditions will become more favourable.

4 The storm has reached its peak. Cling to correct principles and endure it.

3 Anchor yourself to the correct principles of the Sage. Don't worry about opposition from others.

2 Resist the urge to interfere, and have patience. This situation will not last indefinitely.

1 Acting now in response to fear and doubt will end in disaster. Things are as they should be.

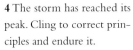

---

24. FU
RETURN
Change, turning
point, improvement

EARTH

THUNDER

Just as the winter solstice presages the returning power of the sun, this hexagram, which is related to that time of year, tells of a time of increasing fortune. It is also a reminder to look for the light of inner truth to help guide your path. In the same way that the seasons progress in an inexorable cycle, so too do the ebb and flow of fortune and misfortune. However, do not be overconfident and press forward rashly, or you may lose the support that has brought this turning point. Watch and wait as things progress at their own rate, and draw in your strength for the time of growth that is approaching.

LINE READINGS

6 Now is the time for careful self-evaluation and for correcting improper attitudes you may find.

5 If you are moved to justify or excuse your behaviour, you are aware that you are in the wrong.

4 In going your own way you may have to forsake or offend others. True friends will understand.

3 Change can be frightening but there is no gain if you keep returning to bad habits.

2 Be careful of allowing your pride to stop you from learning from others.

1 Be aware when you stray from a true and honest path, and return before you go too far.

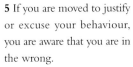

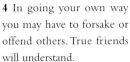

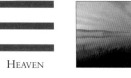

25. WU WANG

INNOCENCE

*Purity, innocence, guilelessness,
sincerity, intuition*

HEAVEN

THUNDER

Innocence is living purely in the present, as a child does, with no thought of tomorrow or yesterday. The innocent child accepts the guidance of the wiser adult and has a guileless trust that all will be well. Develop the innocence you have within so that there is no anticipation of events and no holding on to what has passed, good or bad. The pure, innocent spirit in all of us, the higher self, is directly connected to the rest of creation. If you nurture it, intuition flows and it is possible to follow the guidance of the wiser adult, the Sage, as it leads us through life.

LINE READINGS

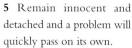

6 Have patience. Do not try to force an issue but step back and let the truth unfold.

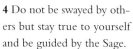

5 Remain innocent and detached and a problem will quickly pass on its own.

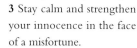

4 Do not be swayed by others but stay true to yourself and be guided by the Sage.

3 Stay calm and strengthen your innocence in the face of a misfortune.

2 Concentrate on the present and do not dwell on past mistakes or future goals.

1 Trust your first instincts because intuition flows from the cosmos and points the way.

---

26. TA CH'U

THE TAMING POWER OF THE GREAT

*Keeping still, tension, practice,
staying firm*

MOUNTAIN

HEAVEN

It is a time to put into practice the teachings of the I Ching. To remain calm and detached in the face of hostile provocations from others who seek to undermine your resolve is a great test of the strength of your character. Hold firmly to the sense of inner truth – the power of the great – during these testing times, and use the difficulties as opportunities to increase your understanding by purifying your thoughts and actions. These attacks may come from people who are jealous and fearful of your spiritual progress, or from inner aspects of yourself that clamour for attention. Pay them no heed and remain focused on who and what you are.

LINE READINGS

6 Creative energy released and guided by your correct behaviour will bring success.

5 Acting out of desire causes great disruption to your equanimity. Stay calm and detached.

4 Curb actions that arise from strong emotions to allow you to know the right time to act.

3 Proceed with determination and caution because there are still problems ahead of you.

2 By staying calm now you conserve your energy for greater advantage when the time is right.

1 Staying calm and patient in a difficult situation will bring a quicker resolution.

27. I

CORNERS OF THE MOUTH

*Nourishment, discipline,
meditation, fulfilment*

MOUNTAIN

THUNDER

The image of this hexagram is a mouth, open and ready to receive nourishment. Just as food nourishes the body, thoughts and actions nourish the spirit. If we take in unhealthy food the body suffers, and if we indulge in unhealthy thoughts the spirit is adversely affected. By feeding on the desires of the ego we promote the growth of inferior spiritual qualities such as envy, self-pity, distrust, and so on. Meditation is a way to cultivate a tranquil, receptive state that allows wisdom to flow from the universe, nourishing our higher selves and influencing others positively as the peace and tranquillity it instils radiates outwards.

LINE READINGS

6 Others turn to you for guidance. Remain humble and sincere in your dealings with them.

5 Strengthen your discipline and follow the guidance of the Sage before you try to help others.

4 You will receive help by seeking to nourish yourself in the proper manner.

3 Feeding on desires is never properly fulfilling because there is always something else far better to be had.

2 Seeking nourishment from others will weaken you and bring misfortune.

1 You have everything you need, cease from striving to no purpose and be content.

28. TA KUO

PREPONDERANCE OF
THE GREAT

*Pressure, regeneration, growth,
cautious progress*

LAKE

WIND

This hexagram indicates a situation of almost unbearable pressure, and it seems likely that you will give way beneath the weight. When we are under intense pressure there is an understandable temptation to escape and seek a refuge, but that only delays the inevitable and sooner or later we are faced with another test. To keep running only weakens our resolve and makes problems seem unbearable. Now is the time to stand firm. You are equal to the task and by relying on your inner truth and integrity you will emerge stronger. This may require a sacrifice on your part to bring a wider benefit to others, but benefits will accrue if you face the test.

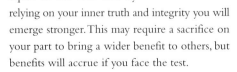

LINE READINGS

6 You are in over your head because of overconfidence. Return to patience and humility.

5 To progress in a renewed relationship the problems that undermined it need to be resolved.

4 Do not exploit the respect that others have for you or there will be great cause for regret later.

3 Stop your headlong rush, which is propelling you towards disaster.

2 This is a time of renewal. Things will go well if you stay alert and proceed slowly and with caution.

1 Be cautious as you advance and test each step. Do not be afraid to pull back if danger threatens.

29. K'AN

THE ABYSMAL

*Depths, despair,
danger, alertness*

WATER

WATER

Flowing water follows the path of least resistance on its journey from the heavens to the sea. The doubling of water indicates depths of despair, dangerous pits and chasms, which are created by giving in to strong emotions that urge us to give up or to seek an easy, immediate solution to problems that might face us. The other depths are those within ourselves which, if plumbed, can provide the strength to see us through difficult circumstances. Flow with the current of change in life instead of struggling against it. Open your heart and adopt the receptive, detached state that will allow the universe to work out the best solution.

LINE READINGS

6 Your predicament comes from ignoring what you know to be right and true. Listen to your heart and follow what it says.

5 A thing will come to fruition when it is ready. Stop striving and go with the flow.

4 Be sincere in all your thoughts and actions, and help will come.

3 Any movement is dangerous. Retreat into stillness and discipline until a solution comes.

2 Slowly and cautiously is the way to find your path through the dangerous abyss that faces you.

1 Be alert to danger or bad habits and return to the path of peaceful acceptance.

---

30. LI

THE CLINGING

*Dependence, passion,
brilliance, intensity*

FIRE

FIRE

Fire gives warmth, illumination and simple beauty, burning with an intensity that is captivating. But fire is nothing without fuel, depending upon wood to give it form and clinging to it with passion. We humans depend on external things for our physical survival, but there is another dimension that gives us a passion for life and that is a spiritual connection to the rest of creation. Just as oxygen gives fire an extra intensity, so spiritual nourishment gives us extra vibrancy. Clinging to correct principles gives us the strength to live a joyful and fulfilling life, able to face difficulties with equanimity and paradoxically to gain independence.

LINE READINGS

6 The ego in its many guises still holds sway and needs to be silenced before progress can be made.

5 Be humble and accepting in the face of adversity, and good fortune will be yours.

4 Perseverance in the correct manner will bring its own rewards in time.

3 Accepting that things come in their own time allows their healthy growth and development.

2 Stay calm. Do not succumb to either despair or over-exuberance. Moderation in all things will bring good fortune.

1 Listening to desires and inferior attitudes leads inevitably to misfortune.

31. HSIEN

INFLUENCE

Harmony, mutual benefit,
coming together, courtship

LAKE

MOUNTAIN

This hexagram indicates the approach of an influence. The constituent trigrams represent the third son and the third daughter, suggesting courtship. This means that you must follow the correct procedure to bring about a joyful union that is mutually beneficial to both the parties involved. To be able to receive benefits from external influences that are working for our good we need to be open-minded and gentle. To have a beneficial influence on others we need to maintain our inner independence and integrity, acting from a position of quiet inner truth and humility.

LINE READINGS

6 Let your knowledge become deeds and they will have a greater influence than words alone.

5 Hold firm to your inner truth but beware of being too rigid.

4 By always speaking and acting with integrity you will have a positive influence on others.

3 Desire can cause you to act rashly or use your influence for selfish gains.

2 Have patience. Correct progress takes time and to act now will lead to misfortune.

1 Maintain a firm discipline in the early stages of an influence and success will come more easily.

---

32. HENG

DURATION

Persistence, progress,
endurance, stamina

THUNDER

WIND

This is a time of endurance, which requires persistence and stamina. By calling upon the enduring principles of calmness, humility and sincerity, and being careful to stay true to your path, you are sure to achieve success. You may be going through a change or perhaps there is one coming, but whatever is occurring, the counsel of this hexagram is to hold your equanimity. Do not yearn or hope for something to be better, and do not fear that things will get worse, but remain constant and unwavering in your actions as you deal with the situation, doing what needs to be done with calmness, detachment and integrity.

LINE READINGS

6 Stay calm and experience the present to allow the creative energy of the universe to work.

5 Do not interfere. Allow others to make their own way, learning through their own experiences.

4 What you seek will not be found if you only look in the wrong places, or in the wrong way.

3 Do not measure yourself against others but remain strong and certain in your own path.

2 Your intuition flows through your higher self. Trust in it to guide you.

1 Expecting too much too soon can only lead to disappointment. Stay focused on the present.

33. TUN

RETREAT

Withdrawal, conserving strength, stillness, order, safety

HEAVEN

MOUNTAIN

There is a natural ebb and flow of energy, which the discerning person recognizes and accepts. Faced with the onset of winter, a tree does not put forth new growth but draws in its strength and waits for spring. When there are superior forces marshalled against us, it is best to retreat into calm stillness to conserve and organize our strength. Retreat is not a disorganized rout, fleeing in panic and desperation. It is acceptance of the fact that you are faced with unfavourable odds, performing a strategic withdrawal in order to make preparations for a more favourable time to advance.

LINE READINGS

6 You are correct in retreating, and your path will open up before you.

5 You have seen the wisdom of retreating now and must act decisively.

4 A correct retreat at this time will only serve to strengthen you.

3 Don't allow others to interfere with your priority to withdraw.

2 A fair and proper resolution cannot come about if you demand it or interfere in the situation.

1 Withdraw from a negative situation now and take no further action.

---

34. TA CHUANG

THE POWER OF THE GREAT

Self-possession, strength, heaven, patience

THUNDER

HEAVEN

This is a time of increasing power and strength, but it is necessary to guard against self-congratulation and complacency. We reach this position with the help of the Sage. In following the correct principles of patience, humility, gentleness and detachment, we align ourselves with the creative forces of the universe and can achieve great things. But it is important to remember the other guiding counsels: reticence, waiting for the appropriate time to act and staying balanced. If, through a misguided belief in our power, we seek to use this influence to benefit our own ends, the resulting misfortune will be great.

LINE READINGS

6 Pressing forward without due consideration can lead to entanglements that will halt your progress.

5 It is sometimes necessary to be harsh but do not carry the punishment too far.

4 If you remain true to your principles, resistance will crumble and good fortune is assured.

3 Use your strength wisely. Be patient and advance when there is no resistance.

2 Gentle persistence will lead to further progress, so keep your discipline even in the easy times.

1 Don't be tempted to use your power to force issues. To act now will bring disaster.

35. CHIN

PROGRESS

Advancement, dawning, rising

FIRE

EARTH

Fire over earth represents sunrise, and this hexagram indicates a time of great progress. The sun climbs effortlessly in the sky because it follows the natural laws of the universe. The growth of our understanding and influence will also be easy if we remember where the light of our brilliance comes from and follow the guidance of the Sage. Clouds obscure the light and power of the sun and, similarly, our judgement can become clouded if we do not keep ourselves and our actions pure and simple. Work for progress for its own sake rather than in the pursuit of selfish goals.

LINE READINGS

6 Treating others harshly to teach them a lesson is an abuse of your power.

5 Progress is not always obvious but by remaining detached you have made great gains.

4 Using your power for selfish material gains will lead to misfortune.

3 It is not weak to receive help. Keep to your path as truly as possible and accept aid gratefully.

2 Don't compromise your principles for the sake of a union.

1 Progress seems slow in coming but keep your faith and gains will accrue.

---

36. MING I

DARKENING OF THE LIGHT

Oppression, damping, inner light, sunset

EARTH

FIRE

Earth over fire represents sunset, indicating a time of approaching darkness. The power and influence of the sun diminish as night encroaches and the only light left is the inner brightness. When we are engulfed by difficult circumstances, it is necessary to keep that inner light bright to help guide us through difficulties. Giving in to weakness or feelings of despair at making no progress dims the brightness within. Now, more than ever, is a time for detachment and perseverance at maintaining an inner truth. Things progress slowly but progress they do, so have faith in the creative power of the universe.

LINE READINGS

6 Hold fast to your true path and firm your resolve, and you will win through.

5 There is no shame in hiding your true self from those who may wish you harm.

4 Realizing you are on the wrong path enables you to leave it. To stay is foolish.

3 Identifying the root of the problem is only half the job. Persevere in dismantling the blockage.

2 Accept aid that is offered and, in turn, be unstinting in your efforts to help others.

1 Detach yourself from a desire for progress and continue with patient perseverance.

家
人

37. CHIA JEN

THE FAMILY

*Harmony, togetherness, loyalty,
health, balance, structure*

WIND

FIRE

For a family to be successful and grow in a positive way it needs a firm structure with a strong, honest leader and harmonious relationships between the members of the group. This togetherness stems from a mutual love and respect for the family members and a loyalty to the group, so that there is a willingness to put the welfare of the whole above individual desires. This firm foundation is essential for the health of all human communities, and needs to start with the individual. By cultivating the correct principles of acceptance, humility, modesty and gentleness we attract and develop healthy relationships.

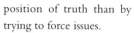

LINE READINGS

6 Good fortune will be yours if you keep your actions and thoughts correct.

5 Your influence will be greater if you act from a position of truth than by trying to force issues.

4 Ensure your actions are for the right reasons and are not based upon ulterior motives or false emotion.

3 Be fair but firm when you are dealing with others. Weakness or aggression towards others will bring misfortune to you.

2 Do not resort to bullying or aggression.

1 Set clear boundaries; if people know their limits they can act more freely within them.

睽

38. K'UEI

OPPOSITION

*Misunderstanding, contrary
resistance, adversity*

FIRE

LAKE

Opposition arises through misunderstandings and this is because people, events or situations are judged by their external appearances. If we feel that circumstances are against us or that life isn't fair because it is not what we expect or desire, we misunderstand the way the universe works. Resisting the flow of creative energy only increases the power of the inferior attitudes we harbour, which in turn increases the resistance in an ever-intensifying spiral. Everything that comes to us is appropriate for our learning and spiritual growth, but this can only be discerned by looking beneath the exterior to the lessons within.

LINE READINGS

6 You feel threatened by others or by life but your paranoia is unfounded.

5 Openness and understanding will allow a firm relationship to grow.

4 Trust in the universe and approach life with an open heart and you will meet other like-minded people.

3 Circumstances may seem to be against you but actually everything is as it should be, so look for the lesson.

2 Understanding can be overlooked unless you receive everyone and everything openly.

1 Accept what comes. Do not chase after things, as that will only drive them further away.

39. CHIEN

OBSTRUCTION

*Obstacles, barriers,
blockage, stuck*

WATER

MOUNTAIN

When we are faced with barriers or obstacles, we are often tempted to indulge in self-pity or to seek to forcibly remove or overcome them. These attitudes brought about the blockage in the first place and only serve to make the obstruction seem even more insurmountable. If we give in to these emotions, we block the assistance of the higher self and progress is not possible. There is no point in seeking to blame others for the predicament; the answers will come from looking within. It is best to retreat from the problem and examine the self for attitudes that need correcting, and to seek advice from a wise friend or counsellor.

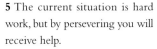
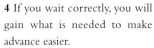
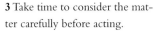
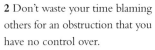

LINE READINGS

6 Others may need your help. Do not forsake them even if the difficulties seem too great.

5 The current situation is hard work, but by persevering you will receive help.

4 If you wait correctly, you will gain what is needed to make advance easier.

3 Take time to consider the matter carefully before acting.

2 Don't waste your time blaming others for an obstruction that you have no control over.

1 Forging ahead at this time will only make things worse. Easy advancement will come when the moment is right.

---

40. HSIEH

DELIVERANCE

*Relief, release,
growth, progression*

THUNDER

WATER

The trigrams of thunder and water together suggest a great thunderstorm that purges and refreshes, and brings new life to the surface. If we look within when faced with obstacles and seek to correct improper attitudes, relief begins. Because of the work you have done on yourself, you are being released and the way is clear for steady progression. Now is a time to step forward with confidence and balance. Don't brood on what has gone but forgive and forget any past harms that have been done, accepting them as lessons that were needed in order to reach this point.

LINE READINGS

6 There is a last vestige of ego preventing complete deliverance. Let it go and be free.

5 Deliverance comes from firm rejection of old habits and inferior influences.

4 Don't cling to old ideas or acquaintances that may halt your progress.

3 Do not succumb to pride and arrogance lest you undo all your good work.

2 Use your wisdom to see through any false praise you may receive. Your progress will be halted if you believe in it.

1 An obstacle has been overcome. Take time to reflect on it and ensure it does not return.

損

41. SUN
DECREASE
Discipline, simplicity, limited, drawing in, restriction

MOUNTAIN

LAKE

Decrease is not necessarily a bad time; it is simply another state in the constant flux of life. Everyone reaches a point where their strength is low and energies need to be garnered to avoid depleting them further, causing a greater imbalance. This hexagram is a timely reminder that a period is coming which requires a return to simplicity. It is a time for restricting the demands of the ego to strive for success or the attainment of goals. Power is limited but, by drawing in and exercising firm discipline, it is possible to rely on the inner strength available to get through the lean period.

LINE READINGS

6 Persevering on the path of honesty and sincerity will bring success.

5 Good fortune will come by following what is true and correct in yourself.

4 If you adopt a humble and sincere attitude you will attract others to you.

3 Releasing inferior elements will allow beneficial aid to come.

2 Do not compromise yourself to help others; to do so will be to the detriment of all.

1 If others seek your aid, give what is asked of you with love and humility but do not over-extend yourself.

益

42. I
INCREASE
Improvement, gain, progress, assistance

WIND

THUNDER

Like decrease, increase is an inevitable state in the endless cycle of changes that characterize life. It will come to a close at some point but now is a time when great progress can be made. When you persevere on a path of correctness, the creative power is called upon and it answers by invigorating you. To continue the progress, beware of complacency and remember the source of your good fortune. Be generous in sharing it with others in a humble and sincere way. This will draw out what is good in them and they will give you their support. Continue to strengthen your inner resolve and be firm in eliminating inferior elements in your character.

LINE READINGS

6 Be generous with your time and energy. It is beneficial to you if you give assistance gladly when others request it of you.

5 Kindness brings its own respect and recognition without being sought.

4 If your guidance as a mediator is sought, be gracious and sincere in the role.

3 Even mistakes turn out well, but heed them and learn from them so that they are not repeated.

2 An open acceptance of the workings of fate means that no obstacles can stand before you.

1 By remaining selfless you will bring the success that you seek.

43. KUAI

BREAKTHROUGH

Resoluteness, determination,
resistance

LAKE

HEAVEN

A breakthrough comes if you are resolute in dealing with the inferior influences of the ego. By resisting emotional responses to other people and situations, it is possible to defuse them before they become too great. To keep emotionally disengaged is to follow the teaching of the I Ching and that allows the creative higher powers to flow, unfolding destiny in a propitious manner. Once the breakthrough has occurred it is necessary to remain resolute, determined not to resort to other inferior expressions such as pride, arrogance or complacency. If these enter, the Sage will withdraw and other obstructions will be experienced.

LINE READINGS

6 The breakthrough has come about and success seems assured. Maintain your discipline to carry it through to the end.

5 Do not judge or condemn others who behave incorrectly; they must make their own mistakes.

4 There is a danger that resoluteness will turn to hardness and intolerance.

3 Do not be provoked into action, even if others urge you to do so.

2 By remaining cautious and watchful, you will see dangers approaching.

1 Be aware of your personal limitations and don't be over-confident.

---

44. KOU

COMING TO MEET

Caution, awareness,
temptation, tolerance

HEAVEN

WIND

"Coming to meet" refers to having an open attitude when meeting with the Sage or with other people, being non-judgemental, sincere, humble and accepting. Acting in this way gives you the ability to deal with any mishaps that may arise calmly and efficiently. There is also a warning here, that by ignoring danger signs it is possible to meet inferior elements halfway and thus allow them to develop from a weak position to one of growing strength. It is a time for self-examination to test the correctness of ideas, situations and potential allies. If your suspicions are aroused, listen to them because they come from the higher self, which knows what is best.

LINE READINGS

6 Withdraw from the challenges of inferior elements in others who are hostile towards you.

5 Trust in your inner truth and cultivate your understanding, but don't use it to berate, convince or impress others.

4 Don't dismiss others out of hand, no matter how offensive they may be.

3 If you feel under attack, retreat into stillness to avoid extending the conflict.

2 Aggressive resistance of inferior emotions will make them stronger as they thrive on attention.

1 Negative influences should be nipped in the bud while they are still weak.

萉

45. TS'UI

GATHERING TOGETHER

Peace, harmony, co-operation,
prosperity, leadership

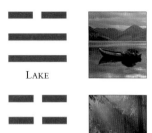

LAKE

EARTH

When a group acts together towards a well-defined goal and in a spirit of peace and harmony, its strength is magnified to such an extent that the whole is greater than the sum of the parts. For such a union to prosper, however, requires a strong leader. To be such a leader means gathering within oneself the principles of correctness in order to be able to deal with the outside world in a calm manner. Acting from a stable base, he or she will transmit their strengths to their followers without words or coercion, but if their inner truth is not sincere that will be sensed and the support will fade away.

LINE READINGS

6 If you are sincere in your devotion to the correct principles, success will be yours.
5 Remain firm in your goals and don't be afraid to go on alone if necessary.
4 Your own success is assured if you work selflessly for the general good.
3 Be tolerant of outsiders, forgive readily and do not hold grudges against someone who has strayed.
2 Join with people you feel naturally drawn to and trust in the creative higher powers.
1 Make sure your goals are of the highest order and not just self-serving aims.

升

46. SHENG

PUSHING UPWARDS

Direction, ascending, growth

EARTH

WIND

This hexagram suggests a sapling growing stronger and reaching higher, and now is a time when great progress can be made by persisting in what is right. Just as a tree starts from humble beginnings to reach great heights, so can you. A tree also stays firmly rooted in its origins, drawing strength from there, which indicates that by maintaining a connection with the Sage, the origin of this success, you will remain strong and firmly rooted. Do not be afraid; simply trust and follow the guidance of the Sage, asking for help from those able and willing to give it. Nothing can stand in your way if you push steadily towards the light.

LINE READINGS

6 How a goal is achieved has as much importance, if not more, than the goal itself.
5 Progress may seem slow but have patience; growth is sure and steady.
4 New opportunities are approaching and success is assured if you maintain your discipline.
3 How far you go depends on how closely you follow the Sage.
2 By sacrificing petty concerns of the ego you will further your growth greatly.
1 The teaching of the I Ching draws you on and by reaching for it and accepting its wisdom you invoke its power to help you.

47. K'UN

OPPRESSION

Exhaustion, stretched,
adversity, endurance

LAKE

WATER

The water is below the lake and therefore the lake is exhausted, dried up, its vital resource gone. These are testing times with difficult situations and little or no progress. Any progress that is possible comes from being steadfast in the principles laid out in the I Ching. Facing this adverse time with calm and equanimity will allow the lake to refill, plugging the leaks that drain away the precious reserves. A great drain on energy and resources, leading to fatigue, is often caused by harbouring untruths, so this is a time for self-assessment. Look within to see if you are being true to your spirit, your path and the Sage.

LINE READINGS

6 The time of oppression is almost over and it is only negative attitudes that hold you back.

5 The oppression is great, but be patient and have faith in the workings of fate to see you through.

4 A closed mind is the greatest oppression, so dispel fixed ideas about yourself or others.

3 The obstacles are within, so look to your attitudes and see what may need correcting.

2 Do not wish for more, but be grateful for what you have and draw strength from it.

1 Resist the feelings of despondency and look within for inner reserves of strength.

48. CHING

THE WELL

Spiritual nourishment, counsel,
guidance, wisdom

WATER

WIND

Water is a fundamental requirement for survival, and the well was a focal point for traditional communities. It was available for all to draw upon and needed to be treated with respect so that it did not become polluted. The image of the well in this hexagram refers to the I Ching as a source of spiritual sustenance that is freely available to any who wish to draw from it. But Ching also serves as a reminder to treat that deep wisdom with respect and not to muddy its waters with frivolous queries or indifference. To gain the full benefits of Ching, you need to draw from it with sincerity and to accept its guidance wholeheartedly and with good faith.

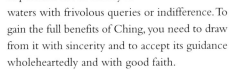

LINE READINGS

6 By selflessly giving of yourself to others your good fortune will be multiplied.

5 Knowledge only becomes wisdom when it is used. Apply your wisdom for the benefit of all.

4 Remain true to the principles of the Sage to maintain the quality of your inner truth.

3 You are avoiding what is right for you. Unused talents are wasted.

2 Don't be misguided. Focus your energy and intent on something worthwhile instead of misusing it.

1 If you neglect yourself, others will also neglect you, so rejoice in who you are.

革

49. KO

REVOLUTION

Change, advance, devotion

LAKE

FIRE

The ideogram represents an animal's pelt in the process of undergoing its seasonal change in response to environmental pressures. Ko signifies that changes are afoot or that attitudes need to be revolutionized to effect the necessary change and progress. Whichever is the case, now is the time to consider yourself deeply, to analyse your motives and instil the necessary change of heart that will set things in motion. Success is assured if you act from a position of selflessness, because this will bring the support needed and give an awareness of the right time to act.

LINE READINGS

6 The major change is done. Now is a time for fine-tuning in order to carry the change on.

5 Actions based on proper principles make you stand out and others will follow.

4 For change to be long-lasting your motives and actions need to be pure.

3 Don't act too hastily or be too hesitant, but retain your balance and pay close heed to your intuition.

2 Prepare carefully before making radical changes.

1 Take time to develop your inner strength before making your move.

鼎

50. TING

THE CAULDRON

Growth, sacrifice, nourishment

FIRE

WIND

Ting derives its name from the image created by the lines of the hexagram. The bottom line is the legs of the cauldron, the next three the belly, the fifth the handles, and the top line the lid or carrying rings. The cauldron was regarded as the heart of a household, providing food and nourishment for all; if the cauldron was full there was sufficient for everyone. This hexagram is related to Ching (number 48) because it is about providing nourishment, but whereas Ching, or The Well, is about the spiritual growth of the individual, Ting is more about developing what is good within ourselves for the benefit of society at large.

LINE READINGS

6 Lead others by your example in being open, honest and gentle.

5 Remain modest and sincere and you will receive help in difficult times.

4 Stay alert to potential dangers and don't take on more than you can manage.

3 Don't look for recognition but be patient; just reward comes in its own time.

2 Don't be over-sensitive. Others may express envy towards your success but that cannot harm you; have confidence in your actions.

1 By acting with honesty and purity of intent, success is assured.

51. CHEN

THE AROUSING

Shock, movement,
stimulation, excitement

THUNDER

THUNDER

Thunder piled on thunder represents the incredible power of nature to pull us up short, to arouse and stimulate. Is it terrifying? Does that initial jolt give way to excitement or are you unperturbed by such momentous events? If you are shocked by external influences, it indicates that there are areas or attitudes that need looking at. The bigger the shock, or series of shocks, the bigger the imbalance that needs to be addressed. The truly powerful person is unmoved by such occurrences, being in complete harmony with the universal laws. Now is a time to look within and determine where self-correction needs to be made.

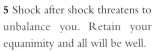

LINE READINGS

6 The shock marks the end of the old. Contemplate ways of making a fresh beginning.

5 Shock after shock threatens to unbalance you. Retain your equanimity and all will be well.

4 All movement is blocked; it is a time for patience, stillness and self-evaluation.

3 Use the shock to open your mind and look for possible avenues of action.

2 Do not be afraid to let go of possessions. What is really important will be returned to you.

1 The shock has come as a lesson. Do not be afraid but accept it gratefully.

---

52. KEN

KEEPING STILL

Stillness, observing, quietness,
clarity, readiness

MOUNTAIN

MOUNTAIN

Mountain after mountain stretching away into the distance is the very image of stillness. Stillness means not allowing the mind to be ruled by strong emotions because it is not possible to be still with a clamouring mind. What is needed is a calm observation, suggested by the ideogram which represents an eye over a person. From a balanced position such as this, observing the emotions but not acting on them, it is possible to gain a clarity that confers a state of alert readiness. The alertness allows recognition of what needs to be done and the readiness empowers you to do it: being still when stillness is required and acting when action is needed.

LINE READINGS

6 You are at the peak of the mountain, allowing perfect stillness and clarity.

5 Excessive talking is a sign of a restless mind. Calm your thoughts and speech.

4 If you keep calm and still inside, external influences will have no effect.

3 Problems will arise from a rigid approach. Don't allow your stillness to become inflexibility.

2 Don't be pulled along by someone else if it doesn't feel right for you.

1 It is easier to keep still before you move. Be cautious, follow your intuition and don't act impulsively or without due thought.

53. CHIEN
DEVELOPMENT
Gradual progress, patience, steady growth

WIND

MOUNTAIN

Wind over mountain represents a lone tree growing on an isolated mountainside. In such an exposed environment the tree needs to have firm roots and to grow gradually and with care, but once it is established it will live long, have an unparalleled view and be visible from a long way off. It is the same for us: to take possession of a fine position and to enjoy the benefits of it, it is necessary to grow gradually, progressing step by step and learning all the lessons that life brings. The goal may seem a long way off but with patience and diligence it will be arrived at.

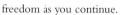

LINE READINGS

6 Your progress is visible from afar, serving as an inspiration to others.

5 Your progress may isolate you but it also brings freedom as you continue.

4 Where you are is only temporary, but take time to relax before you go on.

3 Rash actions will bring regret. Allow things to develop gradually.

2 Your advance is steady and you can feel secure in sharing your self-development.

1 At the beginning of a journey there is often anxiety. Keep your goal in mind and you will progress.

---

54. KUEI MEI
THE MARRYING MAIDEN
Impulsiveness, disturbance, desire, proper conduct, discipline

THUNDER

LAKE

The image called up by this hexagram is that of thunder creating waves on the surface of a lake, indicating how turbulent desires can lead to a disturbance of our equanimity and can often result in impulsive actions. To act on desires is to fail to follow the correct principles as laid out in the I Ching. There will always be desires and problems in relationships, but Kuei Mei counsels that by following proper conduct their effect will be minimized. Proper conduct means maintaining discipline in being detached, accepting and being wary of compromising your principles by following your desires.

LINE READINGS

6 Don't act without thought. You need to be sincere in your words and actions.

5 Don't insist on being in charge. Be prepared to stand back and allow others to come to the fore.

4 Be patient and persevere towards your goal.

3 Don't expect too much too soon. There is no disgrace in starting from a lowly position.

2 You may be let down by someone but don't let this affect your faith in those you love.

1 With the proper attitude progress is possible, whatever your position.

豐

55. FENG

ABUNDANCE

Fullness, power, wise
actions, plenty

THUNDER

FIRE

The trigrams of thunder and fire represent movement and clarity. They also indicate developing an inner awareness to see what position you are in and to move when the time is right. In order to take full advantage of these cycles of waxing and waning power, it is necessary to recognize them and to act only when it is appropriate. While a thunderstorm fills the sky it is full of power, and its influence is felt universally but, like all things, it will pass. Do not look to such a time but live for the present moment, making the most of this period of abundance and influence to achieve great gains.

LINE READINGS

6 Arrogance and conceit towards others will bring alienation and misfortune.

5 You can achieve great things but not without the help of others. Listen to them with respect.

4 Don't get lost in confusion but be guided by your own inner clarity.

3 Hold to your inner truth and nothing can stand in your way.

2 Your influence will shine through. There is no need to pretend to greatness.

1 Your inner clarity will see the time to advance, and your energy will carry you through.

旅

56. LU

THE WANDERER

Moving, restless,
temporary, transient

FIRE

MOUNTAIN

The idea of transience comes from the component trigrams which represent a bush fire on a mountain flaring up and moving along, always seeking more fuel. This can relate to physical travel but it also refers to progressing through life: the best way to proceed on that journey is as if passing through a strange land. When travelling in unfamiliar territory it is wise to be stay alert, to be cautious, reserved and respectful to those you meet, to follow your instincts about places and situations. And also to travel light so that you are able to react swiftly, to carry only what is necessary and to have no attachments.

LINE READINGS

6 Be careful of taking your good fortune for granted or it may be lost.

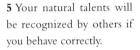

5 Your natural talents will be recognized by others if you behave correctly.

4 You are settled for now but you know in your heart that really you are not satisfied.

3 Direct your energies properly. Don't involve yourself in something that is really no concern of yours.

2 With the right attitude and demeanour you will always find a resting place and friends.

1 Remain free of attachments and trivialities, and your journey will be much easier.

57. SUN

THE GENTLE

*Gentle, penetrating,
wind, persistence*

WIND

WIND

To effect any long-lasting change it is necessary to be like a constant wind blowing gently in one direction. When faced with problems, it is tempting to take vigorous action to overcome them, but violent storms wreak havoc and only stir up the local environment. This hexagram advises gentle penetration to dispel any blockages that may stand in your way (either within yourself or in the form of outside influences). To be consistent requires a well-defined goal to focus on, one that can be aimed at with persistent effort. In this way, changes will be long-term and have far-reaching effects.

LINE READINGS

6 To search too hard for inferior elements will cause disruption.

5 Things may have started badly but, if you are duly cautious, they will turn out well.

4 By adhering to proper principles and maintaining your integrity you will reap great rewards.

3 Dwelling on negative influences gives them more strength. Correct them and move on.

2 Search inside yourself for any negative influences.

1 Gentleness does not mean softness. Be sure in your goal and firm in your intent.

---

58. TUI

THE JOYOUS

*Inner strength, fulfilment,
harmony, joy*

LAKE

LAKE

We are surrounded by imperatives – to make life better we must have this or must do that – but these material gains do not bring lasting joy because there will always be something else to have or do. The teaching of the I Ching tells us that to be fulfilled and to live in harmony we need to devote ourselves to the proper principles of humility, detachment, modesty and acceptance. By doing this we cultivate a harmonious balance and achieve an independence based on an inner strength which means that, whatever the situation we find ourselves in, it can be faced with calm equanimity. That is true joy.

LINE READINGS

6 Following pleasure for its own sake is unworthy of you and will escalate out of control.

5 You are surrounded by inferior attitudes in yourself and others, but do not give in to them.

4 Pursuit of inferior aims brings misfortune. Turn to what is higher for lasting joy and greater fulfilment.

3 Don't be tempted by material gains because they will soon fade away.

2 If you remain sincere in your goal of seeking joy, good fortune will be yours.

1 Release your attachment to material trappings and experience the joy of freedom.

59. HUAN

DISPERSION

Division, dissolution, rigidity, stubbornness

WIND

WATER

Stubborn attitudes can often lead to harshness and rigidity, blocking the acceptance of people and situations in a free and open manner. This in turn leads to divisions and a lack of unity both within the self and with others. If you try and break these fixed ideas forcefully you will do no good because they are strong and deep-rooted, and resistance will only increase their strength. The best way to deal with them is to be like the warm spring wind, which blows gently but with great persistence over the winter ice, dissolving it gradually and allowing the river to flow freely once more.

LINE READINGS

6 Don't focus on negative influences or a dangerous situation will develop.

5 A fresh idea can unite people and dispel negativity and misunderstandings.

4 It may be necessary to sacrifice a short-term goal for a long-term benefit.

3 The best way to deal with your problems is to help someone else.

2 Do not judge others harshly. Understanding them will help you understand yourself.

1 Resolve misunderstandings quickly before alienation sets in.

---

60. CHIEH

LIMITATION

Restraint, moderation, guidelines, boundaries

WATER

LAKE

Limitation is not the same as restriction; rather it means being prudent with the resources that are available. In order to be able to use what is at hand to its fullest potential, you need to have guidelines to follow to prevent confusion. If you know and respect your personal boundaries you will have a greater freedom of expression within them, because you will know how far you can go with your expenditure. On a physical level we cannot live beyond our means, and similarly on a spiritual level it is wise to restrain the desires and fears that are the cause of troubled thinking.

LINE READINGS

6 Relax your boundaries. Severe limitations become restrictive and lead to resentment.

5 Don't enforce limitations on others that you don't follow yourself.

4 Accept natural limitations. Move when you can, stay still when you can't.

3 Be careful of over-extending yourself. You are the one that is responsible for knowing your limits.

2 Do not hesitate; take the next step as the way is clear.

1 Know your limitations and keep to them for now. To press forward at this point is bound to bring misfortune.

61. CHUNG FU

INNER TRUTH

*Prejudice, understanding,
acceptance*

WIND

LAKE

Prejudices colour the way we relate to life, other people and ourselves. It is not possible to reach any kind of understanding if we indulge in such feelings as pride, anger or self-pity. Chung Fu is two-fold, referring to the universal truth, the invisible force that manifests visible effects in life, and the inner truth of an individual which also has an invisible influence, good or bad. The I Ching counsels us to leave emotional responses behind and to try to understand the truth of a situation. By doing so, our inner truth is emulating the universal inner truth and has a positive influence.

LINE READINGS

6 Trying to persuade others will do no good. Look to yourself and lead by example and let others make their own way.

5 If your inner truth is strong it will unite you with others.

4 Do not forget the source of your power when things are going well.

3 To maintain your independence and balance, do not rely on others.

2 Your inner truth, strong or weak, will be felt by others and they will react accordingly.

1 Remain true to yourself. Do not be distracted by others from your inner truth.

62. HSIAO KUO

PREPONDERANCE OF
THE SMALL

Non-action, caution, patience

THUNDER

MOUNTAIN

This hexagram refers to the dominating presence of inferior attitudes (the small), either in yourself or in others, which makes correct advance impossible at this time. When faced with difficult circumstances it is tempting to be assertive and to try and find solutions or to win through, but to act in such a way will only make things worse. The best course to take is one of patient non-action, relying on the correct principles of humility, modesty and acceptance to help you. Difficult times always reappear, and should be seen for what they are: a test of our commitment to the higher principles laid out in the I Ching.

LINE READINGS

6 Pressing forward with something beyond you is bound to bring disaster.

5 Seek help from someone who you know has wisdom and is sincere.

4 Be patient, and trust that the higher powers are working things out.

3 Show proper caution and don't expose yourself to unecessary risks.

2 You have made a small advance; accept it and be content with it for now.

1 Keep your current position. To act now will bring misfortune. Bide your time and wait for a better opportunity.

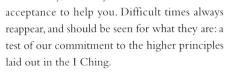

63. CHI CHI

AFTER COMPLETION

*Order, balance,
awareness, culmination*

WATER

FIRE

All the lines in this hexagram are where they should be, and are perfectly balanced; out of chaos comes order, but of course this can change in an instant. Although this is a very positive hexagram, indicating hard work culminating in a time of order, there is a warning not to relax the discipline that has got you this far. It is necessary to be on guard, and to maintain an awareness of inferior elements that may arise and tumble the order into chaos again. If these are not properly recognized and dealt with before they manifest themselves, they will quickly swamp you and undo all your good work.

LINE READINGS

6 Don't look back over past achievements, but keep your eye to the future and move on.

5 Don't complicate matters. Simplicity of thought and action is the best way forward.

4 Minor setbacks are warnings of indiscipline, so pay heed.

3 Maintain your high standards. To revert to inferior attitudes now will undo your good work.

2 Retain a modest and humble heart and mind, and what you seek will come to you.

1 Keep your discipline and self-awareness, and your progress is assured.

64. WEI CHI

BEFORE COMPLETION

*Caution, regeneration,
potential, clarity*

FIRE

WATER

This hexagram is the reverse of Chi Chi (63). There fire is below water and can give its heat to make the water boil; here water is below, moving down, and fire is above, moving up, so the two energies cannot meet and combine. However, the potential is there, and they just need to be repositioned so that fire (which represents clarity) can serve as a base for water (which represents action). During regenerative times such as these there is intense pressure to succeed but, to get anywhere worthwhile, you need to proceed cautiously and with firm dedication to higher principles.

LINE READINGS

6 You have gained much, but maintain your clarity and don't let things go to your head.

5 Maintain your integrity and perseverance and you will meet with success.

4 The endeavour has begun but there is much to do. Dedication is required to reap the rewards.

3 It is safe to act, but seek help if you don't feel strong enough to do it alone.

2 Do not wait idly but prepare yourself carefully for the correct time to act.

1 You cannot move forward safely without clarity. Impulsive actions bring disaster.

INDEX AND ACKNOWLEDGEMENTS

The publishers would like to
thank the following picture
libraries and photographers
for the use of their pictures
in the book:

AKG Photo: 9tl; 11br. The
art archive: 13b; 11tl. BBC
Natural History Unit: 16tr,
bl, br; 19t. Bruce Coleman
Collection: 16tr. Images
Colour Library: 5; 10; 13t;
14bl, tr; 16tl, bl, br; 17. Julie
Meech: 19b. Natural Image:
18b. Tony Stone Images: 3;
6-7; 12tl, tr, bl; 15r, t, b, l;
16tl; 18t, m, b; 19t, b; 20-1;
30-31.